D1401094

Classic
HARLEY-DAVIDSON
BIG TWINS

Mark Marselli

Motorbooks International
Publishers & Wholesalers

First published in 1994 by Motorbooks International Publishers & Wholesalers, PO Box 2, 729 Prospect Avenue, Osceola, WI 54020 USA

Motorbooks International books are also available at discounts in bulk quantity for industrial or sales-promotional use. For details write to Special Sales Manager at the Publisher's address

Library of Congress Cataloging-in-Publication Data Available

ISBN 0-87938-922-2

On the front cover: *The 1980 FXWG owned by Robert Timms, Jr. Kit Noble*

On the back cover: *The 1960 Panhead owned by Tom Mahar. Jeff Hackett*

On the frontispiece: *A 1980 Wide Glide 100ci stroker engine with S&S carburetor, Sifton cam, and dual plug setup owned by Robert Timms, Jr. Kit Noble*

On the title page: *The 1949 Panhead owned by Brendan Mier. Jeff Hackett*

Printed in Hong Kong

Contents

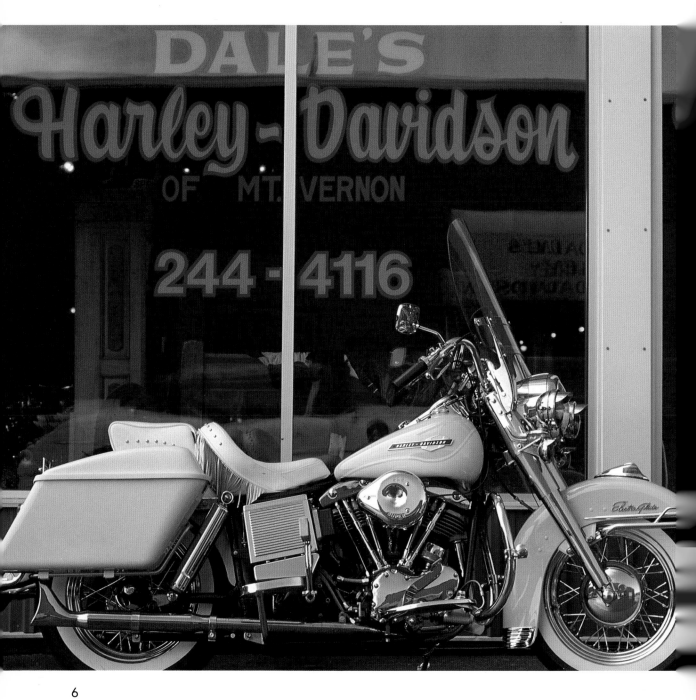

Introduction
Harley-Davidson Heritage and Tradition

More than once I've tried to explain to a non-riding buddy the attraction of a Harley-Davidson and the words never quite seem to work right. It's not that the words are perfect now either, but the more people I talked to for this book, the better I began to understand maybe why it's so tough to explain.

It's hard not to focus on that strong V-twin presence, that distinctive Harley idle, and the vibration that reminds you that you are on one serious piece of machinery. But you can't judge a Harley-Davidson just on that, and you certainly can't explain it in just those terms, at least not if you're trying to capture something about the spirit of a Harley-Davidson.

Beyond what you can readily see, hear and feel is something else that makes a Harley a Harley, and that is two abstract notions called heritage and tradition, overused words that shouldn't be confused with either slick marketing or dusty history lessons. No, heritage and tradition have to do with people with ideas, people who took something and made it better. In this case, it's a Harley-Davidson, a special machine that was built to be ridden, and ridden hard. All you have to do is look at the Knuckleheads, Panheads, and Shovelheads in this book—or go to a bike show or your local chopper shop and see what customizers have done—and you can imagine what it must have been like to get on and ride one during those eras.

While Harley-Davidson have changed over the years—and assuredly will continue to do so—the excitement is no different today than it was 20, 40, 60, or 80 years ago. Easier, yes, but the basic experience hasn't changed. We're just discovering and living a unique experience that thousands and thousands of other riders have already lived. As a wise fellow told me recently, "You get on them and you ride them, and that makes you someone special."

A person could spend a lifetime and then some trying to learn Harley-Davidsons. I'd like to thank Chris Haynes, Ed Rich, Dave Royal, Kurt Heinrichs at the American Motorcycle Institute in Florida, and Skeeter Todd for all their help and also Jeff Hackett for his photography. I'd also like to thank my dad, who rode a Harley or two in his day, and understands my passion for them.

1967 Electra Glide
This 1967 Electra Glide has gotten the aftermarket treatment, from the passenger floorboard to the paint job. Roy Kidney

1 Knuckleheads 1936–1947

Dawn of the Overhead-Valve Big Twin

The sensation of the motorcycle world, the 61 Overhead Valve Twin has gained the praise and admiration of riders everywhere who appreciate the latest in engineering advancements and who demand the utmost in a motorcycle. The performance of this great motorcycle out on the road and in competition, plus its ability to keep going over endless miles, is winning for it thousands upon thousands of new riders every season. For 1939, the 61 OHV is a still finer appearing motorcycle with a new, beautiful tail light, streamlined instrument panel, polished stainless steel fender strips, and attractive color scheme. A number of motor refinements make for still better performance, reduced operating costs, and longer motor life.

Harley-Davidson, Inc.

By the mid-1930s, the Great Depression was waning, but its impact was still felt. In 1935, there were less than 100,000 registered motorcycles in the country, and to put things in even more perspective, two years earlier Harley-Davidson hadn't even made 4,000 motorcycles. No doubt company officials swallowed deeply when they introduced their new 61ci overhead-valve motorcycle in 1936. But Harley-Davidson had weathered bad times, an ability that would prove to be a Harley trademark, and the radically different new model was finally offered to the public. The new model, which was nicknamed the Knucklehead for the distinctive rocker cover nuts that resemble the knuckles of a fist, had been delayed for a variety of reasons. What mattered, however, was that in 1936 the company finally rolled off the lines the most significant Harley-Davidson since the Silent Gray Fellow in 1903.

As dramatic an improvement as the overhead-valve engine was, the first Knucklehead was hailed for its visual appearance as well. The instrument panel integrated into the streamlined gas tank was an immediate hit. The larger speedometer was much easier to read, even if its numbers were on the optimistic side when it came to top-end accuracy. The front of the frame now had a double loop instead of a single one. The rounded

1936 61 OHV Knucklehead
Previous pages, the 1936 Knucklehead was a stunning departure in many ways, but especially in terms of mechanicals and appearance. It was a year of many firsts, and among those that identify the Knucklehead were the distinctive new carburetor intake assembly, the double-downtube frame, the first single-cam engine, and, of course, those rocker covers and nuts that gave the bike its tag. Roy Kidney

Springer fork looked sleeker than the forged I-beams previously used, and the distinctive rocker cover nuts and air intake horn contributed to the bold look. The Knucklehead looked more substantial, more complete than the Flathead it was meant to supersede. It wasn't perfect, but then again, nobody at Harley-Davidson expected the model's first-year production to be without flaws.

The first Knuckleheads were made in limited numbers—somewhere between 1,900 and 2,000—and more than 100 changes, possibly as many as 150, were made by the 1937 model year. Most upgrades were minor although a few were substantial, such as coming out with a heftier frame the next year when the original one proved unable to handle a sidecar; the front downtubes of the frame weren't strong enough to handle the stress. A surprising number of corrections didn't wait until 1937. The distinctive rocker shaft nuts that immediately make you say "Knucklehead" were not on the first models off the line. The original ones were smaller rocker shaft covers held in place by a center screw. The setup leaked, however, and was replaced later in the 1936 production run with the larger nuts. Again, what counted was that the Knucklehead was essentially right, and changes were made as the company learned more about what it had built. It was a different time, a great time to be alive and to ride a Harley-Davidson. And you could ride away on one for the grand sum of $380, an extra $110 if you wanted a sidecar.

"The Knucklehead was a good motorcycle, and it had a good engine," recalled Wally Mitchell, an engineer whose hundreds of patents over the years include the torque wrench. Wally—who is 88 and rode up to his mid-70s—said that riding Harleys back then

1936 61 OHV Knucklehead

Harley-Davidson used to change its gas tank designs on a regular basis, and the 1936 Art Deco style design shown here is considered by many folks to be one of the best that Harley ever came out with. The designs on the preceding VL gas tanks were painted on by hand whereas those on the Knucklehead were actual decals the factory put on. This design was used through 1939, at which time Harley came out with a metal nameplate that was mounted on the tank side. Roy Kidney

was an ever-changing experience. "I even put one in a midget racing car, although that didn't work out too well. We didn't nit-pick about short comings. We were glad for any improvements that were made." It was a good attitude to have, especially for owners of the earliest Knuckleheads. But once the bugs were fixed, the Knucklehead set the standard for the street machine of its day.

It doesn't matter what the era, motorcyclists have always looked for more power, to be able to crack the throttle and command a wicked burst of acceleration. Call it freedom, call it an escape, call it what you will, but motorcyclists tend to have an inherently adventurous spirit. "The Knucklehead I used to ride could out-race anything in the county," bragged Robert Taylor. As a wiry 135lb teenager, the North Carolina man thrived on street racing, and the torquey Knucklehead was the hottest bike then available. The new four-speed transmission featured a constant-mesh system that worked surprisingly well with the new clutch. A rider could adjust the spring tension by turning a nut in the center of the clutch hub.

"It handled pretty well for a big ol' motorcycle. The brakes weren't hardly any good at all, but it was fast. Nobody could beat me," Taylor recalled.

Those were the days when riders would strip the bike, rig the venturi for greater gas flow, and put VL transmission sprockets in for more top end. One hot idea in that era was to run a "square bore" motor, where the stroke and bore were the same, which was thought to give more power. If some ideas didn't work out, others were tried. Some riders even cut down the end of the bike's handlebar grips—anything they thought could get them more performance.

In other words, motorcycling wasn't any different than today, other than motorcyclists of the 1930s didn't have 700-page catalogs from accessory companies packed with goodies to pick from. However, Harley did offer accessory packages from the factory for the first time. You could get the standard set-up with niceties such as a safety guard, a Jiffy sidestand, a lighted speedometer, and steering damper. The deluxe setup included a fender lamp, dice shift knob, and saddlebags and hangers. When it came to the engine, especially for racing applications, what the riders lacked in factory or aftermarket

1936 61 OHV Knucklehead
Left, the dash in this 1936 Knucklehead appears to be from a 1937 model with the speedometer itself from a 1941 and later model. The 1936 model only came with a 100mph speedometer, and it wasn't until 1937 that the 120mph speedometer came out with the tripometer. Also, the silver numbers on black background were not used until the 1941 model year, and that basic look was carried through 1946. It's not unusual to find a 1936 model using a later year part because the original ones are difficult to find. Roy Kidney

1936 61 OHV Knucklehead
Following pages, you can find this 1936 Knucklehead in the American Classic Motorcycle Museum in Asheboro, North Carolina. It was the first of two Knuckleheads received in the state by Creech Harley-Davidson, and it has just 17,000 miles on it. The original owner, Frank Bell, had the Flying Cloud logo hand painted on the cycle. He owned the bike through the late 1970s. His grandson then took it over, and owned it through 1984, at which time the museum acquired it. It is in all original condition with no aftermarket parts, although the rocker covers were updated in the late 1930s. Richard Miller

options they made up for with ingenuity. They pushed them as far as they could go, and if they broke, they tried something else.

Knucklehead riders were fortunate that they had a good engine to work with. Prior to the Knucklehead, Harley's V-twins were side-valve engines. The Flatheads, as they were called, were tried-and-true technology, but they also represented limited technology. The side-valves were mounted in the cylinder itself, not the "flat" head, and the gas-air mixture had to come up sideways through the valves and to the pistons. It was not an efficient system. Part of the firing chamber was in the cylinder itself, so the Flathead ran hotter and it wasn't unusual for the valves to stick. The Flathead was a durable engine, but if you rode it long and hard the pistons could seize.

Enter the Knucklehead. The overhead-valve design allowed the gas-air mixture to go directly to the firing chamber between the piston and head. The fuel mixture could burn better in the smaller, controlled area. And you could feel the difference where it counted: right across the power band. As long as the gearing was the same, a Knucklehead rider could pull away from a Flathead rider any day of the week. Yes, the Flathead continued on (an 80ci model was offered to the public from 1935 through 1941 and you could special order a 74ci side-valve through 1948), but just as 8-track tapes gave way to cassettes—which now in turn have bowed to CDs—a step forward had been taken, and there was no going back. The ohv engine was Harley-Davidson's future.

The 1936 Knucklehead engine had a bore and stroke of 3 5/16x3 1/2in and came in either the E model, the higher-compression EL model with a 7.0:1 ratio, or the ES model, which was geared for sidecars. Instead of a two- or a four-camshaft setup, the Knucklehead engine used a single camshaft with four cam lobes, which proved to be a quieter and more reliable system. The Knucklehead also featured an oil pump that recirculated oil to the top end, instead of the total-loss system, which wasn't really quite as archaic as the name implied. With the total-loss system, the rider kept the engine lubricated by pumping oil from a tank into the engine where it did its job—and better than you might suspect. The oil either burned up or leaked out in the process, and the rider would pump more as needed. That was an art unto itself, a messy one at that, but it worked.

The 1936 and 1937 Knuckleheads had a serious problem with oil escaping from the valvetrain, bad enough that it was difficult for riders to go for even a moderately long ride without risking soaking their pants in the oil. Harley devised a two-piece cup that the

1936 61 OHV Knucklehead
Previous pages, the 1936 Knucklehead featured new innovations from front to rear. Up front was a new and improved Springer suspension, while the front and rear wheels featured a new center hub design referred to as the star wheels, which were totally different from the old-style VL center wheels. The new hub design for the 18in wheels, when you saw them from the side opposite the brake drum, looked like a five-pointed star. Richard Miller

1936 61 OHV Knucklehead
The new Springer, with the sleeker, rounder look (gone was the flat I-beam construction), was accompanied by new handlebars and a newly designed horn. The Knucklehead also came with a new three-piece crashbar that was used for one year only. Richard Miller

valve spring fit into. A high-domed cap was snapped on, with a slot on the side that the rocker arm went through. On the bottom was a vacuum line that fed into the rocker box to remove oil from the valve springs. Thus the oil was kept in check.

John "Spitzie" Splittgerber of New York, a New York Harley-Davidson dealer who was born in 1903 (fate *must* have had a hand in his future) recalled installing the oil repair kits that he used to be call "splatter kits." Riders might not have been happy about the initial oil problems, but they still embraced the new Harley. "The Knucklehead came out, and it was something new and it was definitely faster," Splittgerber said. That was enough, he said, to create a demand that would both make the Knucklehead a success and further cement Harley's position as the Number One American maker of motorcycles. Aside from the initial oil problem, Harley-Davidson had a winner, much to the pleasure of its dealers who had witnessed far less pleasant results when the company came out with its 45ci model in 1929 and its 74ci model in 1930.

The best way to make people want to buy a motorcycle is by showing what it can do, and that's what Harley-Davidson did. In March 1936, riding a specially prepared Knucklehead, Joe Petrali set a speed record

1936 61 OHV Knucklehead
For the first time ever, Harley-Davidson offered accessory packages to riders. On of the touches you could get was the dice shifter knob on the hand shifter. And no, that's not a hand clutch on the lefthand grip. The front hand brake was located on the left grip side through 1951 when they went to the hand clutch. The reason for using the left grip? It allowed riders to gas with one hand while leaving the other hand free to brake. Richard Miller

of 136.18mph at Daytona Beach in Florida. The next year, a superb rider by the name of Fred Ham settled any doubts that the Knucklehead could handle the long haul. In 1937, he went to Muroc Dry Lake in California where he circled a 5-mile course for a one-day period on a new Knucklehead. Over the next 24 hours, Ham rode 1,825 miles, a stunning feat for any rider—either then or today—on any machine, either two wheeled or four. Ham averaged just over 72mph, and more than 83mph for the actual time he was riding. He set 43 AMA records during his marathon session, his only repair being the replacement of the rear chain. The Knucklehead was a proven commodity.

The Knucklehead's fundamental design was sound, enough so that "the engine has been the basis for everything that's happened since," observed Chris Haynes, a former Oregon Harley-Davidson dealer with a passion for Knuckleheads. What made the Knucklehead even more of a home run was that at the same time, arch-rival Indian came out with its trouble-prone "Upside-Down" Four model, which would prove to be one of its least successful bikes. "Harley was smart with the Knuckle and lucky with Indian," Haynes pointed out. "I've heard people say that it's better to be smart than lucky, but if you can be both, that's even better."

The Knucklehead was a remarkable machine, and when you talk to people whose passion is knowing as much as they can about them, you begin to realize just how incredible it was. One such person is Ed Rich, who recently opened the American Classic Motorcycle Museum in Asheboro, North Carolina. One of the Harleys housed in his museum is the 1936 Knucklehead shown here. When you ask Rich about the Knucklehead,

1936 61 OHV Knucklehead
It's roughly six decades old, but the technology used in the Knucklehead engine can still be seen in current Evolution engines. The design has been refined over and over, but the basic layout of the Knucklehead's overhead-valve engine is still the heart of today's Harley. Richard Miller

1936 61 OHV Knucklehead
Here's the grandfather to the Fat Bob gas tanks
that Harley-Davidson uses today. The Motor
Company had used a two-sided tank before this,
but one of those two tanks was used for oil.

This 3 1/2-gallon tank was the standard size tank
used through 1964. This original bike is worth
more in this condition than if it was restored.
Richard Miller

the history gushes forth like water from a faucet.

"The 1936 Knucklehead featured a double downtube, which replaced the single-loop frame that had been used previously. It was one of many changes that were good, but not perfect. The frame proved too fragile for sidecar use, especially the two downtubes that went from the neck casting down to the rear of the bike. The frame was beefed up for the 1937 year, and would be further beefed up over the years. The 1936 Springer front end had a new rounded look that was standard through 1948. The bike had wide Buckhorn bars, and the '36 was the only one where the damper control was on the driver's right side. The shifter gate on the 1936 was also a one-year offering, featuring a round shifter arm, which in following years was flat. The tank panel integrated in the gas tank was considered a masterpiece. The speedometer read 100mph with or without trip, while later ones had 120mph with a trip. The front and rear wheel and hub lugs were longer through 1939, and the early 1936 model had a hole through them so you could use safety wire to prevent them from backing out. The 1936 taillight, which first came out in 1934, was known as an Air Flow. It was a hooded type, and was used through 1938.

"Neutral was between second and third gear in 1939. That was very odd and it didn't last but one year, and may even have been changed during that year. In 1939, the Cat's Eye dash came in, and the next year, 1940, was the first time they had a metal badge on the sides of the tank. The 1940 frame was the first year they put the teardrop-shaped toolbox high on the motor mount. In 1941, the frame went from a 28-degree rake to a 29-degree rake. That was done to help the handling for the 16in wheels, and on the early 1941 models that was done by bending the frame at the factory.

"The Linkert carburetor was used up through 1965 with only minor variations. The carb name and venturi size may have changed, but the carb was basically the same. You could get an engine guard, better known as crash bars, in a three-piece setup. Two sides bolt to the sidecar loops (there's also a small brace between the sidecar loops going to each side to keep the frame from flexing), and where the crash bar connects it goes up and fits into a third clamp-type piece that clamps the two ends together. The 1936 models had a one-year brake system that featured a very small rear brake drum that simply didn't have enough stopping power. You could get 5.00x16 tires as an option on the 1940 models, and the wider tires gave you a better ride."

The history goes on and on, and so would Ed if you didn't stop him to ask what was so special about the Knuckleheads. Then he starts explaining how the Knucklehead put Harley-Davidson in the engineering forefront. Arch-rival Indian no longer could lay claim to cutting-edge technology. It was really that simple. Build a better motorcycle, and motorcyclists would buy it. It didn't have to be perfect, and it wasn't: the Knucklehead was simply the best there was at the time. Today we laud it for its historical significance and beauty, but back then it was something

1936 61 OHV Knucklehead
The 1936 Knucklehead was the first four-speed Harley-Davidson and featured the first recirculating oil system. The oil tank was located on the center of the frame behind the center downpost (you can see it just above the kickstarter). Another first was the flex pipe cover used on the exhaust. Richard Miller

else. It was a motorcycle, and it was meant to be ridden.

"We were kids. So what if they bucked like all hell? That was the state of the art back then and we figured we were lucky to have it," said Dave Kenny, parts manager at American Harley-Davidson in Leominster, Massachusetts, who owned a 1938 Knucklehead. "We used to say, 'I went on a two-pack ride,' meaning two packs of gum, because if you went

1940 EL Knucklehead
There's a lesson in the virtue of waiting behind this 1940 EL, which was parked, in sad shape, in the proverbial barn in 1976 when Bob Gagne of Maine first saw it. He was able to get it started but the owner wasn't ready to sell. He asked him to call when he was ready, and a full decade later he finally got a call. Gagne restored the Knucklehead with the help of Don "Pappy" Heath. Jeff Hackett

100 miles and didn't go through a couple of packs of gum the vibration would break your teeth. Part of the reason was the roads and highways back then, which were paved with concrete. Every 25ft or so there'd be a tar strip that connected two sections, and you'd hit it—'Ba-boom.' The ride would be a constant series of 'Ba-boom, ba-boom, ba-boom.' Lots of riders wore kidney belts with their names on them. Bandannas were in, and nobody wore helmets—what were those?"

The big seat may look comfortable, and the idea of a post taking the shocks sounds good, but not everyone loved it, Kenny said. "A lot of guys would just pull that puppy out of there and ride on the frame. You might sit on a pad. A buddy of mine used bath towels. It got you down lower." Riding on unfamiliar roads at night was serious work, even though the Knucklehead's headlights were said to be better than Indian's. "The headlight was like a candle in a windstorm," Kenny said. The rear light was so weak that the Knucklehead was almost invisible at night from the rear. "There weren't any aftermarket companies for us to go to. That's all there was. It wasn't as if the 6-volt system could have done much more anyway," he said.

"Getting the brakes to work was awesome," Kenny said. Every time you hit the brake it was a challenge to see if you were going to stop. You didn't have a front brake, so to speak, so we used to stand on that rear one. God help you if you had to hit the brakes in the rain." One thing Kenny and some of his buddies tried back then was to scuff up the soft brakes. Not only did it not help much, the brakes they were scuffing up with sandpaper and blowing on were made of asbestos. "Who knew about that stuff back then? It didn't help much anyway," he recalled.

1940 EL Knucklehead
In 1940, you could buy a 61ci EL Knucklehead like this one for a little under $500. It was the first year for the metal tank badges and riders could also get optional 16in wheels. It was a slow time for the Motor Company, which built a total of 10,461 Harleys that year. In the Knucklehead era, you rode a handshifter because that's what they came with. First gear was all the way forward, then neutral, second, third, and fourth (other than 1939, when neutral was between second and third, a one-year-only oddity). Owner Bob Gagne said that he had an interesting time trying to master the handshifter the first time because he was in a field where he had to dodge both cows and cowflops. Maybe it's because he didn't hit anything, but he learned to love a handshifter. Jeff Hackett

Phyllis Buzzini, who today runs the Alaska Silk Pie Co., a gourmet pie shop in Alaska, still vividly recalls riding on the back of her boyfriend's 1938 Knucklehead in the 1970s. They used to take it everywhere, but the ride at times was so bumpy that she insists that the following is true, and not as odd as it sounds. "He used to lash my hands together in front of him so I wouldn't fall off." Harley-Davidsons have a way of bringing people together, whatever the era.

By 1938, one messy problem that had been improved was the oil system. The oil had

1940 EL Knucklehead
The goal was to restore this bike as near to stock as possible. Bob Gagne went with a custom windshield windscreen, and if you look at the other photos, you will also notice that the paint is Wimbledon White, the tires are replacements from Coker, and the saddle bags aren't original; they're from a 1990 Heritage Softail. Bob was getting the original ones restored when these photos were taken. Jeff Hackett

seeped pretty freely from the valves, which now were fully enclosed with a cover over each one. The earlier models could be retrofitted although some grinding was necessary. The frame was bolstered even more and the clutch assembly was upgraded. Riders grew up on the hand-shift, foot-clutch setup, and like anything else, if that's what you're used to, it was what was right and likely preferred.

"It was a real thrill riding a Knucklehead," recalled Roy Bokelman, a former Harley dealer who remembered well the days of the Flathead. "I was used to riding the Flatheads, and going to a Knucklehead was great. It felt like it had twice the power. It was smooth and had great torque. It was a real bouncy ride, but we didn't care."

Bokelman, who as a youth topped 6ft and weighed a solid 225lb, said that he never had a problem kicking his Knucklehead over. The key, he said, was to keep the bike well tuned. "As long as you reset the points, say, once a month, and kept a sharp eye on the timing, it was easy to start the Knuckleheads. " He noted that being a mechanic, he had no trouble, but woe to riders who neglected their Harley and liked to go for long rides. Back then, motorcycles came with real tool kits and nobody considered that an option. You rode, you carried tools. Most Knucklehead riders were pretty good at the basics, he said. At least they were if they expected to ride. "Not just anyone could ride back then," said Bokelman, admitting that very fact was also part of the attraction.

The 74ci Knucklehead engine came out in 1941, and Harley-Davidson claimed that its new stroke and bore, 3 7/16x3 31/32in, could produce up to 48hp on regular fuel and nearly hit 100mph. The Knucklehead did have a respectable top end for the roads of its day, but again, the Harley speedometers of yesteryear were, shall we say, "quite optimistic." Harley-Davidson historian Harry Sucher noted in his book, *Harley-Davidson: The Milwaukee Marvel*, that he took his 1950 FL out for a hard ride and the speedometer showed 88mph when he was actually doing 75mph. He later convinced a factory representative to come clean: the rep explained that Harley-Davidson felt a "generous" speedometer was in the best interest of riders, especially those tempted to crack the century mark. That held especially for those on later FLH models with the leading-link fork, which could exhibit speed wobble at 90mph. Whatever, Harley-Davidson is not the only motorcycle company that had a speedometer with an unlikely top end, and more than one motorcycle manufacturer today still has speedometers with optimistic top ends when it comes to three-digit territory.

The 74ci Knucklehead was more powerful, but it was also less reliable than the 61ci model, Ed Rich said. "The bigger you go, the more you blow," he noted. The 74s had more vibration because there was more to

1940 EL Knucklehead
The 61ci engine was fine for cruising along at speeds of 60–65mph, reported owner Bob Gagne, who says that starting the Knuckle is a simple case of two priming kicks followed by an

ignition kick. He and his wife Anita enjoy riding it two-up ride, but the ride can be tough on long trips. "The seat can turn you into a soprano," he declared. Jeff Hackett

1947 Knucklehead

The year 1947 marked the last run for the beloved Knucklehead. Its overhead-valve engine, which replaced the side-valve engine, had cemented Harley-Davidson's position as the American motorcycle. Doug Mitchel

crank, and the 61s were smoother riding. But that didn't matter so much. The 74s had more power, and just as they were later phased out by the 80ci engine, so went the venerable 61ci mill. "Vibration is a matter of opinion anyway," Rich observed. "Part of the Harley experience is feeling the ride. Some bikes are so smooth that you might as well be on a sofa." Nobody could accuse a Knucklehead rider of being a "couch potato." The Harley was a demanding machine yet as long as you treated it right it would "ka-chug, ka-chug" along.

The Knucklehead is a reliable, long-lasting motorcycle as long as it is properly taken care of, Chris Haynes insisted. "You can't expect to get 100,000 miles from it like the Evos, but certainly you could get 50,000 miles," he said.

A Florida man, Gerry Lyons, has started a registry for 1936 Model EL Knuckleheads, and at last count he has tallied 122 separate listings, which range from restored Knuckleheads to choppers to a few listings that are just for the engine casings. Lyons, who has been a field judge for the Antique Motorcycle Club the last ten years, said that oddly enough, the Knucklehead didn't get its tag until the Panhead was built, when it was necessary to be able to distinguish the two overhead-valve Big Twins.

The 1941–1946 Knuckleheads were basically the same, largely due to World War II, which understandably drew center stage. Harley-Davidson was busy supplying motorcycles for the military, but non-military models were also made, although those were for police departments and people who could show they needed them for transportation to a war-related job. In the early years, the frame components were fitted together and brass was used to "sweat" them together. When

1947 Knucklehead
This 1947 was restored by Pete Bollenbach, who spent 400+ hours bringing it back to original condition. Doug Mitchel

1947 Knucklehead
The foot clutch's days were numbered, but lots of basic motorcycle ideas, like floorboards, haven't really changed over the years. Harley-Davidson has long operated on a basic principle: Keep it simple, keep it practical. Doug Mitchel

1947 Knucklehead
One testimony to the durability of the 1947
Knucklehead was that even though Harley-
Davidson did not manufacture many of the

Big Twins—1947 production totaled 20,392,
which included the side-valve models and 45ci
twins—many still survive. Jeff Hackett

1947 Knucklehead
The postwar era was a tough time for Harley-Davidson because the demand was there but the company couldn't build enough motorcycles to meet it. Jeff Hackett

brass became scarce during the war, mild steel was used to weld the joints together.

The price for a Knucklehead was still relatively cheap, at least by today's numbers. Yes, if you factor in the value of the dollar it's probably another story, but who wouldn't want to go in the way-back machine and

1947 Knucklehead
Right, the little black switch box by the front downtube housed the three-brush generator that controlled voltage output, although it was not a voltage regulator as we know it. It was still a time of tight resources, and the primary cover and exhaust were not chromed. Jeff Hackett

1947 Knucklehead
There's no doubt about it: This is a rigid frame, and as much as some riders swear by them, it would take a hardy person to hop on that thin seat and ride cross-country. But, of course, that's exactly what people did back then. Jeff Hackett

1947 Knucklehead
Here's a sight you don't see on Evos—the leftside handle grip was set up to retard the timing. Motorcyclists had a regular procedure to go through kicking their Harleys over back then, and woe to the rider who forgot the order. Jeff Hackett

snap up a 1946 Knucklehead with sidecar for the princely sum of $501.92?

Today, of course, it's no small expense acquiring a Knucklehead. Good luck trying to find one of the proverbial Harleys in the back of the barn. The folks who own Knuckleheads have a pretty good idea of what they're worth—a lot. Beyond that, even if you can find one for a decent price that needs work, restoring it requires a lot of time, skill, and money, and that order changes depending on what your abilities are and what kind of restoration you want.

Pete Bollenbach, whose specialty is restoring Indians, restored the 1947 Knucklehead shown in this book. Time? A mere 400 hours to set things right. He said that most of the problems when you get a restoration can be traced back to one of the greatest killers of motorcycles: the careless mechanic. "Our job is to repair and fix those problems. The

more fingers that there were in the pie screwing things up, the worse it is," he said.

It's easy enough to admire the Knucklehead and then ride comfortably away on your Evo, thinking that it's nice to be around today. But Wally Mitchell put it into perspective. "Harleys today don't do anything more than they used to do," he insisted. "You get on them and ride them, and that makes you someone special. Of course, it took a little more nerve to ride them back then," he said with a touch of pride.

1947 Knucklehead

Right, the Knucklehead was designed to be a practical machine in an era when there were relatively few places a rider could count on for help. Crash bars may not be glamorous to look at, but they were there to protect both machine and rider. The toolbox was an essential element, and the wheels were interchangeable. Jeff Hackett

2 Panheads 1948–1965

The Perfect Blend of Form and Function

Harley-Davidson, Inc.

Every one has their favorite Harley, but you can make a good case for the Panhead being the most visually perfect Harley ever built. Proof? Just look at the Heritage Softail introduced by Harley in 1986. The Softail reproduces the Panhead's classic styling. Evo owners can even get rocker covers for their engine that copy the distinctive ones on the Panheads. What's that old saying about flattery? You can safely say that no other motor vehicle's design is as enduring and commercially successful as Harley's Hydra-Glide and Heritage Softail—and if you doubt that, try and remember the last time you saw Ford or Chrysler come out with a 1949 lookalike.

The first Panhead came with a rigid frame, handshifter, kickstart, and a suspension that Messrs. Harley and Davidson would have found quite familiar from their early days. It also had a front brake that wasn't good for much of anything. By the time the last Panhead was made in 1965, it had rear shocks, footshifter, electric start with 12-volt electrics, and a hydraulic fork. It also had an improved front brake, although it still wasn't good for much of anything. Oh well, progress takes time, and Harley-Davidson was then and continues to be known today as a conservative company when it comes to change. Yet in that regard, there were remarkable changes by the end of the Panhead era.

The venerable Knucklehead was retired in 1947, but its overall styling was still there on the first Panhead, although the 1948 model had more chrome. The big difference was in the engine, which featured new cylinder heads made of aluminum alloy, with aluminum-bronze valve seat inserts and steel valve guides. The 74ci engine was not necessarily more powerful than its Knucklehead

predecessor, but it was lighter by about 8lb and had new pushrod-type hydraulic lifters that handled the heat better. There weren't any external oil lines, and an improved oil pump provided more oil up top. The engine featured a new camshaft, exhaust ports, pipes, and an intake manifold that was fabricated from brazed tubing. And of course, there was that distinctive one-piece cover that fully enclosed the rockers and valve mechanism and gave the Panhead its tag. It was truly a stunning machine.

Harley-Davidson has a history of making cautious steps, and so it was with the Panhead. The frame was redesigned in 1948 to handle the taller engine. The new wishbone frame had bowed downtubes and also featured an anchor boss that would be used for the steering damper the next year. So, while the first-year Panhead was known for the engine changes, you could also see the prep work there for the 1949 Panhead, which marked the biggest change in Harley suspension since the introduction of the Springer fork in 1907.

1948 Panhead
Right, for the most part, the first-year Panhead wasn't much different than its predecessor, the Knucklehead. The Panhead shared the same headlight, horn, fender light, and even fender trim. The black Springer front end is correct; chrome Springers are largely an invention of the 1980s. Jeff Hackett

1948 Panhead
Previous pages, the 1948 Panhead was a refinement of the Knucklehead, although numerous visual changes were on their way. The most telling difference to the Panhead engine was the distinctive pan-shaped rocker covers that gave the bike its tag. Jeff Hackett

Knuckleheads had a reputation for bouncing all over the place on bumpy roads, which were a staple of the time. It was part of the package that riders expected. That changed with the introduction of the new

1948 Panhead
One of the few visual changes on the 1948 Panhead was the speedometer. The Knucklehead featured a black and silver face whereas the first Panhead speedometer was blue with white numbers. Jeff Hackett

Hydra-Glide front end, which featured internal fork springs and hydraulic damping. It was a solid, more substantial looking unit, and besides the cleaner appearance it provided a better ride than the old Springer. Front wheel travel was increased by 100 percent, and the telescopic fork, combined with the post seat and wider tires, gave a smoother ride. This was a serious long-haul machine, designed for the rough road system that riders faced.

The handlebars were now mounted on risers instead of being one piece with the top triple tree as in the old Springer, so riders could adjust the bars up and down. Riders weren't talking about ergonomics back then, but being able to set your bars for the optimum position was a step in that direction. Another change you would have to rate as a "sort of" plus was the larger front drum brake, which admittedly was still not much to brag about. Still, the folks who rode them said they were a definite improvement over the older Springer unit that *nobody* depended on. The new fenders had deeper skirts and the stainless-steel side trim and rib had been eliminated. The new model name, Hydra-Glide, referred to the new fork and was the first of three names given to Panhead models.

"I always liked the older style motorcycles," said Luke Karosi, a Connecticut man who owns the 1949 Panhead shown in this book. "They're definitely not as smooth as an Evo, but I'd much rather wrench on an older bike. They're a lot easier to fix, more or less. I also like the handshifter. Once you get used to it, it's second nature. I'd rather have that than a footshifter."

Karosi said that one thing he found odd at first was having to move the transmission to tighten the drive chain. While he praised

1948 Panhead
Here's where the revolution—or evolution, not to steal a later engine's name—began. The 1948 Panhead engine featured aluminum heads and was lighter than its iron-head predecessor. The new hydraulic lifters represented a major change, the advantage being that the hydraulics were quieter than the solid lifters and required less adjusting once they were set. Jeff Hackett

the Hydra-Glide front end, he admitted that he was also surprised just how jolting the ride can be. "They don't call it a 'rigid' for nothing, although it does keep you a lot more alert looking out for bumps." The ride is smooth up until about 60mph when the engine starts to complain, he said. Still, it is a

stable ride, and because there is no swing arm to sway, the rigid frame tends to track well through corners. "The vibration does come up through bars, but it's one of the things I enjoy about it," he said.

In 1950, the black paint was left off the aluminum lower fork legs, giving a polished-metal look to the front end. The Knuckle-head's rocket-style muffler was replaced by a smooth-looking, mellow-sounding silencer that was more in keeping with the style of the new Hydra-Glide. Steel D-rings were added to help seal the Pan covers and end the dreaded oil seepage. The next year, 1951, saw the replacement of the 1947–1950-style tank emblem with the

Harley-Davidson name in metal script and underlined with a separate metal strip. The three small chevrons from 1949–1950 on the rear fender were replaced by a single large piece on each side of the taillight.

"The 1949–1957 Panheads were uncluttered, perfectly balanced," said Dave Royal, a Grover Beach, California, man who makes his living restoring Panheads (his business is

1948 Panhead
The Panhead was generally a solid performer on the highway, but it still had the harsh ride characteristics of the Knucklehead because of the Springer front end. While not perfect, the spring seat was pretty good at soaking up the

nastiest bumps, but riders still had to beware of the sharp jolts and shocks up their arms and shoulders courtesy of the Springer front end.
Jeff Hackett

1949 Hydra-Glide
What a difference a year makes! The 1949 Panhead was pretty much the same as the 1948 when it came to the drivetrain, but from a visual point of view it was drastically different. One of the most noticeable changes was the fenders. Gone were the welded ribbed fenders, and in their place were the new one-piece stamped units. Jeff Hackett

1949 Hydra-Glide
This was the first year that Harley used a name to designate a model. Up to then, Harley had relied on model codes, such as the EL, but with the 1949 Panhead, Harley called it the Hydra-Glide, which referred to the new front end. Gone was the Springer, and in its place was the new telescopic front end, which worked so well that the internals remained virtually the same through 1977. Jeff Hackett

called Panhead Fever, which recently built a Panhead for the Harley-Davidson Cafe in New York City) and uses them for both everyday transportation as well as trips to Sturgis, South Dakota. "I sold a Hydra-Glide to a designer once and he said it was the most beautiful bike he had ever seen."

The Panhead covers were an especially dynamic touch, not only attractive but functional. "The Knucklehead's top end had a way of leaking, but the Panhead had those great big covers that sealed everything,"

Royal said. They leaked the first year because they didn't have the D-rings, but when they put those in and people buttoned them up right, oil didn't seep out, he insisted. He also disagreed with critics who insist that Panheads have an inherent tendency to leak. "That may happen after you put on 30,000 miles, but I haven't had that problem with the ones I've built here," Royal said.

A long-time Harley tradition was shaken in 1952 with the introduction of a footshifter, a move that was not necessarily hailed by riders who had been weaned on handshifters. The handshifters would be around for a long time though, through 1978 to be exact. The footshift setup included a ratchet shifter on the left side of the transmission top and a hand-operated clutch lever on footshift models. The hand lever actuated a booster setup, which came to be called the Mousetrap. This booster required less effort to operate the clutch actuating arm via a cable. The Mousetrap was no longer needed after 1968, when longer, softer clutch springs were introduced. Dave Royal said that this was also another case of where if you treated your Harley right, it would be fine, but if you were careless there would be a price to pay. The Mousetrap could be tricky to adjust, and if it you didn't get it right, pulling the clutch in—or getting it to work at all—could be quite a problem.

Shifting gears in the Panhead was not a slick click, click, click affair. A deliberate approach was needed, and it didn't take long for a rider to learn that the best way to shift was with a hearty thwack. What mattered was that it worked. The year 1952 also marked the retirement of the venerable 61ci engine, which was phased into a past chapter of Harley history by the more-powerful 74ci engine that came out in 1941.

1949 Hydra-Glide
The Panhead engine remained largely the same, although the lower end was upgraded over the years. The top end oiling was better once the oil flow to the lifters was improved. Jeff Hackett

The Panhead was considered a solid engine, but that didn't mean it was left alone. If problems were recognized, they were fixed. Maybe not instantly, but everything was part of a long, gradual refinement process. For instance, the hydraulic units for the lifters were located at the lower end of the pushrod from 1948 to 1952, which eventually was judged to be a mistake. The oil that drained down from the rocker area was too hot for the lifters, and it was also possible for contamination from the upper end to foul the lifters.

The design was changed in 1953 so the hydraulic setup was moved to the lifters, and the oil feed went directly from the oil pump via a filter screen that had been incorporated into the right case. By the way, good luck trying to tell a 1951 Panhead from a 1952 or a

1949 Hydra-Glide
Owner Brendan Mier with his 1949 Panhead. Some folks insist that the 1949 Panhead was the classiest looking Harley ever, and for proof point to the new retro-look Heritage Softails, which capture that yesteryear look. Jeff Hackett

1953. Each shared the same tank emblem and came in solid colors, although if you see a foot shifter you know it can't be a stock 1951.

"The Panheads were OK, but when we got them from the factory it was common for riders to put 2,000 miles on, and then we'd tear them down, and rebalance the flywheels and bore out the cylinders," recalled C. E. Hodde, who runs Aggieland Harley-Davidson in Texas. "When we bore the cylinders out, we'd fit in oversize rings. If you bored it 0.010in over, you'd put in rings 0.020in over. That worked real well." The ride was still rough, but it was part of the experience, he said. "It depended on your age and condition. If you were fit and strong, you were OK, but you had to have a good constitution for a long ride. A lot of guys liked that tough image, the Marlon Brando stuff."

The biker's outlaw image was firmly stamped on the public in 1954 with the release of the Brando movie, *The Wild One*. Even though Marlon wasn't riding a Harley (he was on a Triumph), the movie that was loosely based on an incident in Hollister, California, gave the non-riding public a bad taste towards motorcyclists. "That was a real low point for the image of motorcycling," recalled Harvey Ferrell, a North Carolina rider who started riding in 1946 and is a lifetime HOG member. The reality was far different. Nearly every city had a club, and come Sundays a dozen or more guys would get together and ride out to the races on their Harleys. AMA Gypsy tours and rides to Sturgis and Daytona were the big deals. "It was a fun thing, a together thing," Ferrell insisted. "Nothing like those movies."

One Harley rider said that when the movie came out, a local theater owner invit-

1949 Hydra-Glide
The 1949 Panhead featured aluminum heads, hydraulic valve lifters, and a one-piece pan-shaped cover that fully enclosed the rockers and valve mechanism. Change was gradual yet slow after this drastic reworking, a Harley trademark. Jeff Hackett

ed Harleys owners to come and park their bikes out in front. About thirty Harley owners showed up and they went to the movie, not knowing what the storyline was. "We were shocked," he recalled. "That movie really changed the way the public looked at us. Until then, they had always looked at us as if there was something odd about us, but it definitely got worse after that movie came out. It was a real sore spot with us."

Harley's 50th Anniversary was held in 1954 instead of 1953, which would have been fine if only someone could explain why the 90th was celebrated in 1993 instead of 1994. Whatever, the 1954 Panhead was commemorated with a medallion on the front fender and a number of special paint jobs. The plaque read "Fifty Years" across the top, "Harley-Davidson" across the middle, and "American Made" across the bottom. That

47

1949 Panhead
The front of this 1949 Panhead rides on a 1948 Springer that the owner, Dave Monahan of Minnesota, insists came stock, one of 50 or so built that way. Harley-Davidson was not known for throwing parts away, so it is possible that a 1949 with a 1948 Springer front end may very well have been a reality. Jeff Hackett

1949 Panhead
The big news for 1949 was the new Hydra-Glide front end, which offered double the suspension travel of the old Springer forks as fitted to this 1949 Panhead. The Hydra-Glide's damping system was a vast improvement over the Springer. You could also order your bike with rubber-mounted handlebars, which mounted on risers and allowed riders some adjustment— ergonomics years ahead of the times.
 Jeff Hackett

year you could order anniversary Yellow and Daytona Ivory. The special paint offered that year included: Pepper Red tanks and Daytona Ivory fenders; Glacier Blue tanks and Daytona Ivory fenders; Forest Green tanks and Daytona Ivory fenders; or Daytona Ivory tanks with fenders in either Pepper Red, Glacier Blue, or Forest Green. The line under

the tank script was eliminated in 1954. The sharp-looking trumpet horn replaced the round horn that had been used since 1931. The round horn had been moved to the frame downtubes just below the tank mount in 1949 with the advent of the Hydra-Glide front end. The wishbone frame was replaced in late 1954 with the famous straight-leg

1949 Panhead
The rocker covers did tend to leak on the 1948 and 1949 models, which did not have the D rings that were first used in 1950 and, when properly mounted, put an end to the oil seepage some critics loved to point out. Jeff Hackett

frame. At this time, the front engine case guard was changed back to the Knuckle-head-style crashbar. Hard plastic saddlebags were first introduced in 1954, and leather bags were offered through 1957.

Roy McNish of Kingston, Ontario, vividly recalls how he came to buy one of the first anniversary bikes. It was June 1953, and he

1947 Knucklehead and 1949 Panhead
Previous pages, two different eras of Harley-Davidson overhead-valve Big Twins, the Knucklehead and the Panhead. Still, there really isn't a lot of visual difference, as you can see here. Both of these bikes belong to David Monahan of Minnesota. Jeff Hackett

was parked at a raised bridge that was in the process of going up to let a big ship by. A Harley rider pulled up on a new Panhead. "I was sitting there on my little foreign bike, looking at this big beautiful Harley, and I asked him where he got it. He told me, and I turned around and rode to the dealership and ordered one then and there. It cost me $1,495 Canadian."

When the Harley finally came in, McNish had a surprise—nobody had told him that the leather saddlebags that he admired so much had been replaced. His bike was the first one in Canada to come with the hard saddlebags. "We always had leather saddle-bags, and I didn't know they had changed it," he said. "At first I thought they were real-ly ugly, but I liked them later on. Anyway, there were twenty people around, and the dealer told me to start it. I was 5ft, 6in and weighed 128lb. I kicked it down about halfway and it kicked me back up and almost over the windshield. I didn't expect that kind of compression. But once I learned to ride that bike I loved it. It was great."

It's hard for riders today to judge the Panhead because it was a different time. The average road was twisting and turning, not

1949 Hydra-Glide
Right, Luke Karosi with his 1949 Panhead, which had sat rusting away for years in a Texas barn after the owner died fighting in Vietnam. The father finally decided it was time to move some memories along and Luke ended up with the Harley. The Panhead needed a total restoration. The rear fender was so rusted that the tailpiece fell off when the bike was lifted. There was no engine, so Karosi started with a set of STD cases and built himself a Panhead engine. He tried to keep it as stock as possible visually, but did opt for 12-volt electrics and all Andrews gears. Jeff Hackett

1958 FLH Duo-Glide
The end of an era came in 1957 when the last of the rigid-frame Big Twins rolled off the assembly lines. The 1958 Duo-Glide marked the introduction of rear suspension. The Duo-Glide name was impossible to miss on the front fender. Ironically, however, in recent years the rigid look has become more popular than ever. Richard Miller

the kind of place for high-speed blasting. The Panheads cruised easily at speeds of 55–60mph, and several riders noted that you

1949 Hydra-Glide
Left, for years, motorcycles came with tool kits, and riders were expected to know how to use them. Purists will have to forgive owner Luke Karosi's "Lady Luck" touch; the bike did have a sad past, but finding and restoring it definitely was a lucky touch. Jeff Hackett

never needed to look at your speedometer because your engine told you when you were going faster. The Panhead was smaller and lighter than today's Dressers, and McNish admitted that he was one of the Harley riders who couldn't resist a flair for dramatic entrances by hitting the brake and spinning the rear wheel to the curb. Back then, riders didn't think twice about riding their Harley through fields like a dirt bike, he said. The seat was low enough for even a

short rider to touch the ground comfortably, and even though the Panheads were big bikes in their day, they weren't top heavy with extras like Tour Packs and stereo systems. "The bikes were ideal for the roads we rode on back then. You couldn't ride them 1,000 miles in a day, or at least you wouldn't want to, but the Panheads were every bit as good then as the Dressers are today," McNish said.

Harley made a lot of styling changes in 1955. The tombstone taillight was replaced by a squarish unit with rounded corners that looks similar to today's taillight when viewed from behind. The chevrons on the rear fender were eliminated and the tank emblems were replaced by a fancier script that featured a sweeping stylized V at the front of the emblem. The new handlebars featured cleaner twist grips and the four horizontal ribs on the upper front fork cover were replaced by three 45-degree ribs. A new smoother outer primary cover replaced the diamond cover that had been around since 1936.

A new higher-compression, hotter-cammed engine was introduced in 1955 and was designated the FLH. The lower-compression engines were designated FL (civilian) and FLE (police). The FL designations used for Harleys in this era were: FL, FLH, FLE, FLEF, and FLHF. The final F designated footshift; the lack of an F designated handshift. Dave Royal noted that the actual numbers stamped on Harley engines contain all the appropriate letters except the final F, so you can't tell by

1958 FLH Duo-Glide
This low-mileage 1958 Duo-Glide is on display in the American Classic Motorcycle Museum in Asheboro, North Carolina. Richard Miller

1958 FLH Duo-Glide
The 1958 model year also featured the hydraulic rear drum brake, which was new for two-wheelers, although Harley-Davidson had offered it on three-wheeled Servicars since 1951.
Richard Miller

1958 FLH Duo-Glide

Up through 1957, Harley-Davidson's rear fenders had always been supported by braces that mounted to the frame near the rear axle. But the rear suspension and swing arm changed all that.

Chrome fender struts that ran from the back of the top rear portion of the frame now supported the rear fender. Richard Miller

looking at the engine number whether the bike was a footshift or a handshift model. Harley reportedly built only 50 to 200 handshift FLH models a year from 1955 to 1964, but since Harley didn't stamp that final F, Roy-

al said some folks mistakenly think that it was the footshift FLH models that were rare.

The milder handshift FLEs were dropped after the 1956 model year. Police use accounted for much of the FL handshift pro-

1960 Duo-Glide Police Model
This 1960 Panhead started out as a police bike and served 10 years in Detroit before it was retired and auctioned off. The new owners let it sit in basket form for 20 years before Joe "Oz"

Osborne came along, bought and restored it. The Panhead still has the original cases, headlight, taillight, fenders, Linkert carburetor, and hydraulic front fork. Jeff Hackett

duction because the milder-tuned FL engine was less prone to overheating when left idling for long periods. Also, the handshifter allowed an officer to stop and leave the bike in gear with the clutch disengaged while using his left hand to stop traffic. Some funeral escorts still use handshift models for this reason.

The lower end was beefed up in 1955. The engine cases were redesigned to take new bearings. The left side used a Timken bearing that proved so satisfactory it wasn't changed until 1969. The right side was a smaller caged roller bearing that was replaced in 1958 with a larger, stronger caged roller bearing. The old screw-on intake manifold nuts were replaced by an O-ring and clamp setup that was less likely to leak air. The thin steel D-rings that held down the Pan covers were replaced by thicker cast-aluminum D-rings. Those new D-rings were secured with six bolts, but it still wasn't enough to prevent oil seepage around the covers. The next year, 1956, the setup was changed and twelve bolts were used to hold the covers down. Many 1955 models were retrofitted. That same year, 1956, saw the return to the two-tone tank paint scheme; the last standard two-tone tanks had been offered in 1939. Also new for 1956 was a brighter, easier-to-read speedometer face, a higher-lift cam, and a new increased-flow air filter. It was also the first year for the optional rear exhaust crossover pipe, dual mufflers, and directional signals.

The 1957 was significant because it was the last year of the rigid-frame Harley Big Twin, although some of the lighter bikes continued to have rigid frames into the early 1960s. It was also the last year for the 32E generator introduced in 1932. It had proved tolerable for civilians but inadequate for

1960 Duo-Glide Police Model
The two-piece aluminum combo headlight bracket and fork cover were introduced in 1960. The handlebars were now made of two pieces that slid into the sides of the handlebar mount, which was hidden by a triangular-shaped aluminum cover. Jeff Hackett

police use once radios were added in the mid-1930s. A two-brush generator capable of a greater power output and an automotive-type current and voltage regulator was developed for police use, a redesign of which replaced the three-brush generator on civilian models in 1958. A higher-output, fan-cooled generator was continued on police models.

The next year, 1958, saw the introduction of a Panhead with a swing arm-mounted rear wheel with damper units that gave it suspension both forward and aft. Just so nobody would miss this new feature, the bike was renamed the Duo-Glide, and a nameplate to that effect was mounted on the front fender.

1960 Duo-Glide Police Model
Another "new and improved" feature for 1960 was the frame-mounted Buddy Seat, which was flat and relatively narrow. Shorter riders must have welcomed it because the seat height had changed considerably (read that "taller") with the new rear suspension. Jeff Hackett

The name Hydra-Glide continued to appear on the upper front fork cover in 1958 and 1959; Harley may have done that either to denote the name of the front suspension or simply because it still had a supply of the fork covers.

That same year, 1958, also featured the introduction of the rear hydraulic drum brake. Some riders insist that they worked better than some of the early disc brakes Harley later used. Whatever, the hydraulic brake was a revolutionary step in the motorcycle field, at least for two-wheelers (Harley's Servicars had had hydraulic brakes since 1951). The new sidecar also had a hydraulic brake that was

connected to the bike's master cylinder with a tee on the rear brake hose, which in turn allowed both brakes to be simultaneously actuated with the bike's rear brake pedal. The right engine case was redesigned in 1958 to take a larger caged bearing, a move that worked so well it was used into the 1980s. New engine guards, called crash bars by most riders, were introduced.

Slow but continual change continued to be a Harley trademark. Harley's rear fenders had always been supported by braces that mounted to the frame near the rear axle from the earliest bikes right up through 1957. Once the swing arm was used, that had to be changed because it moved independently of the rest of the frame. Chrome fender struts that ran back from the top rear portion of the frame now supported the rear fender. The new optional luggage carrier bolted directly to the fender struts. Prior to 1958, it had been necessary to drill holes in the rear fender to mount the luggage carrier.

For 1958 only, standard paint schemes included two-tone fenders with the tank panel color, Birch White, on top of the fenders. This resulted in the top of the tanks being a different color than the top of the fenders in all of the two-tone paint schemes. It also caused some grief for folks trying to track the right paint combination down years later.

New, optional bumpers were introduced in 1958, featuring a "V" at the front and rear of the front and rear fenders, and were a popular enough touch to run through 1966. New pot-metal fender tips and tank emblems replaced the plastic items in 1959. The fender tips had a diamond-shaped center that matched the "V" in the new bumpers. The tank emblems were shorter than the metal emblems from previous years and featured an arrowhead in front of the

Harley name. And not that a lot of people noticed, but a motorcycle company called Honda was advertising a 50cc bike, announcing something about meeting nice people.

A two-piece aluminum combination headlight bucket and fork cover was introduced in 1960. The top triple tree had the riser mounting holes closer together than the earlier Hydra-Glide front end. The two tall risers used from 1949 to 1959 were replaced by a lower one-piece mount. The handlebars were now two piece and slid into the sides of the handlebar mount, which was hidden by a triangular-shaped cover. The Hydra-Glide name no longer appeared on the motorcycle.

A frame-mounted Buddy Seat was introduced in 1960, available in red and white, black and white, or solid white. It was flat and narrow, and offered a lower seating position than the sprung seat, but some riders found them uncomfortable. The addition of rear suspension had raised the seating position considerably and this seat was probably offered because of demand from shorter riders. You could also get a Super Deluxe Buddy Seat in black and white or red and white. After 1965, the smooth seat got a waffle-like pattern.

Aside from having the lower end improved in 1955, the Panhead engine remained essentially unchanged over the years, and that was good for the owners. Just about any part from the engine—pistons, rings, rockers, valves, rods—could be swapped with another one if it was the same size. Riders took advantage of that flexibility too. There may have been lots of changes over the years, but the Panhead was known for being a motorcycle you could work on. All you needed were some basic tools and a modicum of wrenching ability, which a rider then was

1960 Duo-Glide Police Model
For a company with a conservative reputation, Harley-Davidson has long showed a willingness to experiment with the finer touches, such as the look of its gas tanks. This arrow tank badge may not be quite as stunning as some of the early Art Deco looks, but it fit the feel of this 1960 Panhead. Jeff Hackett

expected to have.

It was all part of the experience. Harley never divorced itself from its past. Never has, never will. When other motorcycle manufacturers started rolling in new blueprints and models, especially in later years, all of a sudden riders found that they had obsolete machines. Harley-Davidson didn't do that. If something worked, you used it. And sometimes when something didn't work right, you tweaked it a little so it would work right, and you could continue using it. The hydraulic lifters used from 1953 to 1984 (part number 17920-53A) are the same; the clutch hub assembly used from 1936 to 1984 (part number 37550-41B) is the same, although the clutch plates can be different, but the shell and hub aren't. The replacement Timken

1965 FLH Electra Glide
The first Panhead came with a rigid frame, handshifter, and kickstart; by 1965, the Electra Glide was introduced and it was the dawn of a brave new world in Milwaukee. This FLH is owned by Tom Mahar. Jeff Hackett

neck (part number 48315-60) was used from 1960 to 1988. That's what you call interchangeability.

A dual-point distributor and dual coils were introduced in 1961. Later that same year, a timing mark was added to the left flywheel for the rear cylinder. On the early dual-point models you had to use a special gauge to measure piston position to time the rear cylinder. If you didn't have one, you had to pull the rear head to do it. Harley figured

that it was much simpler to add the rear timing mark. The dual points and coils were used through 1964. Theoretically, the dual points should have allowed more precise timing, but they were hard to adjust and often were replaced with the earlier single-point and single-coil system.

When the Panhead was introduced, the top-end oil feed was through holes that ran through the barrels. Once the engine was at full operating temperature, the oil reaching the rocker assemblies was extremely hot, which resulted in a shorter life span for the top end. It wasn't until 1963 that Harley remedied this by returning to outside lines. This proved to be effective and many earlier Pans were retrofitted with the new heads.

One Achilles Heel that drove Harley riders crazy was their machine's appetite for speedometers. From the introduction of the Knucklehead in 1936 through 1961, Harley's speedometers had been geared to turn 2000rpm. In 1962, that was changed to 1000rpm. The numerals were also printed on the metal faceplate instead of the underside of the glass as had been the practice since 1948. The tripometer was also changed, increased by one digit. No longer would riders be limited to a 99.9-mile ride. The country—or 999.9 miles of it—was now theirs for the having.

A lot of cosmetic changes were made in 1963. Rectangular fiberglass saddlebags were offered, and today's saddlebags aren't all that much different. Of course, the earlier models did have a few growing pains, such as a tendency for the latches to pop open and let the saddlebag lid fly off. Directional signal lights from 1956 to 1962 had consisted of four small lights and a single red indicator mounted on the riser cap until 1960, when it was moved to the back of the alu-

1965 FLH Electra Glide
The big news for 1965 was the end of having to kick your Harley to life. Going to an electric start meant switching from the tiny 6-volt battery to the huge 12-volt unit. Gone as well was the kidney-shaped oil tank, replaced by a new rectangular oil tank with an internal filter.
Jeff Hackett

1965 FLH Electra Glide
The new Electra Glide looked much wider than the 1964 Pan it replaced, due in part to the switch from the 3 1/2-gallon tanks to the 5-gallon gas tanks. The oil tank and battery also stuck out more, adding to the feeling of heft. While the kickstarter was no longer needed, it remained standard equipment for another two years.
Jeff Hackett

minum headlight cowling. The new turn signals of 1963 were much larger in diameter and of a flattened design with only a slight curve to the back. The front signals were amber and mounted at the bottom sides of the headlight cowling. The rear signals were red and mounted on a one-piece aluminum bracket that bolted to the rear fender under the taillight. That bracket has remained virtually unchanged in the 1990s, other than being widened in 1973 to meet federal regu-

lations about the minimum width between lights.

While all this was going on, the trend to customizing bikes was getting bigger business. Harley riders took to kicking the front ends out with long Springers and saying good-bye to front brakes and front fenders. More aftermarket parts were available to riders. Needless to say, these were straight-line machines, and the emphasis was on looks. The fishtail mufflers were introduced in 1963 as a dual-exhaust option. Harley only offered them from 1963 to 1967, but an idea that works, works, and today you can see fishtails on many new Evos. In 1963, Harley also used a much larger chainguard and offered a wider rear brake drum and shoe. The new brakes could also be relined, whereas the 1958–1962 brake shoes had to be replaced as a whole unit. Other than the yearly change in tank paint scheme and colors, the 1964 Duo-Glide was unchanged from 1963. Likely, Harley was putting its efforts into the Electra Glide, which would be introduced in 1965.

Stats are hard to find, but a 1964 *Cycle World* road test noted the following: The FLH weighed in at a hefty 690lb, but the 73.7ci engine (1207cc) was able to run a respectable quarter-mile time of 15.8 seconds at 83mph. Top "practical speed" was reported as 97mph, but the torquey Harley was capable of going from 0–30mph in 2.5 seconds; 0–40 in 3.8 seconds; 0–50 in 6 seconds; 0–60 in 8.1 seconds; 0–70 in 11 seconds; and 0–80 in 14.7 seconds. Again, the FLH was a hefty bike, a machine meant for riding long distances comfortably.

As *Cycle World* noted, "There is so much torque that the rider can, once he gets rolling, simply poke it into top cog and leave it there.... [T]he engine will haul the bike and its rider up to 80mph in an astonishingly short time without bothering with such trifles as downshifting. With this machine, Harley-Davidson has proved that enough torque is very nearly the equivalent of an automatic transmission."

"Let's face it, you ride a motorcycle for adventure. Owning a Panhead gives you that more than any Evo could," Dave Royal said. The tires were interchangeable. You could put your 5.00in wide Goodyear on the front or you could put it on the back. No doubt there is a computer program that can show how wrong that setup was, but at the time it was a practical approach in an era when being practical mattered, and being able to rotate tires was just that. Today you hear safety experts harping about the need to keep your tires properly inflated. Back then, lots of riders preferred to run relatively low tire pressure because it helped give you a smoother ride.

The final Panhead year saw the introduction of the Electra Glide, which as the name implies was an electric-start motorcycle. Foreign brands had offered electric start for several years (even the little Honda had an electric start), and Harley-Davidson finally came out with its own. The first starter had some growing pains, but it was soon reworked and proved to be a reliable system. Lots of Harley-Davidson riders preferred to kick their bikes to life, and some riders looked at electric start with disdain. "Nobody liked it when it came out," Roy McKnish said. "We hated it because we worried what would happen if it didn't work. Back then, we took our bikes to places you'd never take a car to. If you had a dead battery, how would you get the bike out? With a kickstart, you could always get the bike started. Even if you flooded it, you

could kick it over. It just took more time." That was one way to look at it, and certainly some Harley diehards did, but as the years went by the ease of bringing a bike to life with a stab of the thumb won out, much like the footshifter did over the handshifter.

The Electra Glide looked much more massive than earlier Panheads. The 3 1/2-gallon gas tanks were dropped for the wider 5-gallon gas tanks, although the handshift bikes kept the smaller tanks until the next year when Harley changed the handshift bracket that mounted to the frame so the larger tanks could be used. The oil tank and battery now stuck out on each side of the frame. The engine wasn't changed much, but the stamped-steel inner and outer primary chain cover were now cast aluminum. The new transmission case had mounts cast into it to connect the aluminum primary solidly to the transmission. The inner primary had to be immovable because the electric starter was mounted to it and produced considerable torque when it spun the 74ci engine over. Before 1965, the primary chain had been adjusted by moving the transmission back and forth on its frame mounts. That was now done by a shoe that moved up and down in the primary cover. It was attached to the inner primary cover midway between the motor sprocket and clutch assembly.

An electric start meant that more juice was needed, so Harley went to a 12-volt system. That change spelled the end of the old horseshoe oil tank that had wrapped around the 6-volt battery. The new oil tank, a larger rectangular system, was on the left side. Optional oil filters had been external on civilian models from 1948 to 1964. The new tank featured an internal oil filter. The new 12-volt battery, huge compared to its predecessor, went to the right side, which made it tough to mount the tool kit that now was available only on parts order. The dip in the frame in front of the top shock mounts was eliminated. The frame now had level pieces running from the seat post back to the shock mount, which allowed more vertical room for the electric starter. Everyone has heard those war stories about someone who went to start the bike and forgot to retard the timing and was figuratively "kicked over the handlebars." One rumor even had a biker paralyzed by a kickstarter with an attitude (hyperbole and motorcyclists are on good terms). Anyway, to cure that woe, the manual advance distributor was redesigned to an automatic advance unit.

The Electra Glide was heavier than the Duo-Glide, and wasn't real popular with the go-fast crowd, and the kickstarter continued to be standard equipment through 1967. The kickstarter's popularity has never completely died out, and you can still order kits from the aftermarket. Back then, a rider had to be careful that his or her leg didn't hit the edge of the battery when trying to kick over the engine. A starter relay was added in late 1967 when there was a problem with too much current passing through the starter switch and burning it up; smart riders with an earlier model retrofitted theirs. One other change wasn't such an improvement, at least not aesthetically: Harley replaced the stylish trumpet horn with a smaller unit that was hidden inside the headlight cowling.

The Panhead was never built in large numbers, generally averaging under 6,000 units per year until 1965, when nearly 7,000 were made (2,130 FLs and 4,800 FLHs). You can still find them for sale, but don't expect to walk away with a steal, especially if you are looking for a stock Panhead. Customizing had begun to become popular during the Panhead era, but it would become even more so during the Shovelhead era. When that happened, a lot of Panheads were called into action with front forks 18in over, sky-high pullback bars, sissy bars, and Shovel heads on Pan bottoms. Who needed a front fender? Who needed a front brake (a move that was little noticed, some cynics might note)? In other words, finding a Panhead in stock condition today is no simple task. Little did Harley purists suspect just how far the customizing craze would go, and who would eventually take the lead.

1965 FLH Electra Glide
Right, the final-year Panhead was a fine example of Harley's slow progression over time. By the day when the last Panhead was made in 1965, it was a more rider-friendly bike, with rear shocks, footshifter, electric start with 12-volt electrics, sealed and enclosed primary chain, and hydraulic front forks. Jeff Hackett

3 Shovelheads
1966–1984 1/2

*Factory Customized
Big Twins*

FLH·1200 This is it! Nobody can take you hig... Because no one else has 74 cube... power packed into a four-stroke, V-twin. It's always read... run. Wherever freedom is. Without worries. It has a full-... oil system, new "Security System" cycle alarm, 12-volt a... nator, solid-state rectifier/regulator resistant hydraulic disc brakes, front... and exclusive fa... instrumentation is standard. and rear. Comp...

The Shovelhead era was definitely a time of ups and downs for Harley-Davidson, which came closer than it ever had before to shutting its doors. But it was also an amazing era in that, despite the stormy AMF years, foreign competition, and production woes, it not only survived, but came out stronger than ever, with an expanded product line born of a little mix 'n' match wizardry.

The Shovelhead marked a major change—the widespread embracing of the customized Harley. Yes, riders had long been altering Harleys, but the Shovelhead furthered that approach for the simple reason that it was much more workable. "The Shovelhead became the backbone of the aftermarket business," observed Pete Giannettino, owner of Longriders Custom Motorcycles in Milford, Connecticut. Giannettino, who has built more than thirty frame-up customs, most of them Shovelheads, said that "the Knuckleheads and Panheads weren't as good at being able to take the abuse that riders gave them."

1968 Electra Glide
Right, the 1968 Electra Glide was a hefty bike, weighing in at well over 750lb. It was a smooth-running machine on the highway, but no doubts about it, this was a big machine. The 1968 featured a new oil pump and warning lights for oil, generator, and ignition. This one was restored by Paragon Locomotion in Deerfield Beach, Florida. Gerhardt Heidersberger

1969 FLH Electra Glide
Previous pages, this 1969 FLH has the big fiberglass saddlebags but not the bar-mounted fairing that came out in 1969. The fairing came in white and matched the saddlebags. It was the last year for the serrated header covers, which were replaced the next year by chrome headers. Jeff Hackett

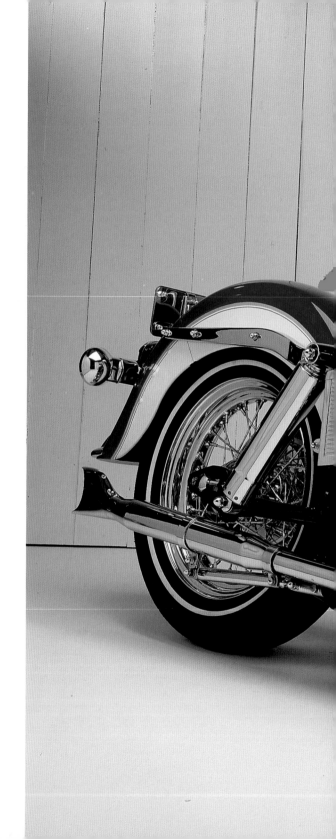

1969 FLH Electra Glide

Jim Glazner of Alabama, who owns this 1969 FLH, describes its ride as "like a big old Cadillac, kind of like bouncing on big bedsprings." The first time he hit a good bump, he went up in the air, the spring seat under him. The megaphone mufflers aren't stock, but they do look good. Jeff Hackett

The first Shovelheads were little more than a Panhead with a different upper end. The Panhead was prone to oil leaks if not treated well, but just as it was better than the Knucklehead, so it went with the Shovelhead, which proved to be better than its predecessor. The Panhead had a strong lower end, so Harley-Davidson focused on the top end. The Shovelhead engine was both stronger and quieter, and when treated properly—something that didn't always happen—it was better on oil control. The cylinder head had a

1968 Electra Glide

The Electra Glide was an elegant if not especially agile touring machine. Its engine was rated at 60bhp, and it was capable of a top speed near 100mph although what was more important was that it could cruise all day at 60–65mph.
Gerhardt Heidersberger

1969 FLH Electra Glide
Does the oval air cleaner look familiar? Harley-Davidson switched air cleaner styles back and forth over the years. The 1969 was the last of the generator Big Twins, and the flat-sided cam cover you see here was gone the next year.
Jeff Hackett

better port design so the engine made more power. The exhaust flange arrangement was improved and the heavy cast-aluminum rocker boxes reduced oil leaks.

The Shovelhead cylinder head was basically an iron Sportster head scaled up and cast from aluminum. They shared the same valve angle, combustion chamber shape, and spark plug locations. The rocker arm assembly was similar (both use a 1.43:1 ratio) and they even shared the same manifold. Aside from the upper end, the only other real change in 1966 was the relocation of the top of the oil feed line from between the tappet blocks to the rear of the right hand crankcase.

"The great unwashed love to fault the Shovelhead for being an oil-leaker, but the truth is that a *correctly put together* Shovelhead engine doesn't leak oil," insisted Kurt

Heinrichs, co-author of *What Fits What on a Harley-Davidson* and *Special Tools for Harley-Davidsons* and chief instructor at the American Motorcycle Institute in Florida. Of course, putting a Shovelhead together correctly meant using good gaskets, clean surfaces, and a torque wrench, a combination that more than a few backyard wrenches didn't employ.

The Shovelhead saw change both in mechanics and in function. In 1966, riders could get a touring package that included a windshield and plastic saddlebags. A few years later, in 1969, you could also get a handlebar-mounted fairing that encompassed the headlight, and a Tour-Pak, a third case atop the rear fender to go with your saddlebags. This was serious space. The Dresser had arrived, and touring became more practical than ever.

When it came to feeding the Shovelhead engine, several different carbs were used with varying degrees of success. In 1966, it was the Linkert Model DC. It wasn't the brass Model M Linkert that had been around since the 1920s, but a whole new carburetor made of die-cast zinc, hence the DC tag. It was replaced the next year by the Tillotson pumper-type carb, which was supposed to be easier to tune. Instead it turned out to be pretty roundly despised. The Tillotson didn't deserve its reputation for being a troublemaker—what it really needed was a good fuel filter as scores of Tillotson carbs caused problems when water got in them. Because they were made of aluminum, the carburetors oxidized internally, resulting in much unhappiness for owners and a bad rap on the carb.

The Bendix/Zenith carburetor came along to the Big Twin in 1970–1971. It proved to be a good unit, and still is popular today although it was phased out, as the story goes, because Bendix wanted to raise the price so much that Harley couldn't stick with it. In 1976, the Keihin carburetor was used, and it proved to be a working carb for the right price. The Keihin wasn't the save-all, do-all everyone had hoped for, but most of the problems associated with the carb stemmed from emission control problems instead of poor design. Today, a Mikuni 40mm flat-slide or Mikuni 38mm round-slide carburetor is a good replacement.

1969 FLH Electra Glide
It's odd to see two sets of directional lights like this. This Shovelhead could have been a police bike that had its flashers changed at a later date. But since we're dealing with Harley history, which has a way of making lots of people look foolish, the key phrase there is "could have been." Jeff Hackett

The Tillotson carbs may not have been beloved, but the first Shovelheads certainly were. When *Cycle World* reviewed the 1967 Electra Glide, it declared it "without equal" in the long-distance touring field. Its test showed the Electra Glide had a top speed of 98mph, was rated at 54bhp at 5400rpm and could finish the quarter mile in 14.7 seconds at 88mph. It weighed in at a hefty 783lb (gas tanks half full), which with a selling price of $2,100 worked out to less than $3 per pound.

The Electra Glide did get a few black marks. It was faulted for the rear shocks for being so close to the swing-arm pivot that it had a tendency to oscillate around corners. And then there was the front brake, a mechanical unit that has been around since 1949, which was described as "laughable," although the reviewer noted that the rear brake did do a pretty good job considering what little help it was getting up front. One ironic mention had to do with the early Electra Glide starter, which had been used on outboard boat motors; it had to be replaced because it turned out to be prone to water damage and corrosion.

The 1966–1969 lower end was, for all intents and purposes, a late-style, 1958–1965 Panhead lower end. The first real change came along in 1970 when Harley-Davidson went to an alternator and employed a completely different set of crankcases. The right-hand case had no provision for mounting a

1970 FLH
This 1970 FLH, owned by Mike Carty, is not a totally stock runner. But adding personal touches, such as a sissy bar, different seat, air cleaner, carburetor, and custom paint job is part of the Harley experience. Jeff Hackett

1970 FLH

The movie Easy Rider may have sparked the custom bike movement, but it was the Shovelhead's technological advances that made it possible for ordinary owners to customize their machines. It also sparked an aftermarket sector that has continued to thrive. Jeff Hackett

generator, so a permanent magnet-type alternator was mounted to the left-hand crankcase. A new timing cover, dubbed the "nose cone cover," replaced the former cover. The old-style circuit breaker also disappeared, replaced by a set of points and a centrifugal advance mechanism on the timing cover that drove off the end of the camshaft. The left-hand flywheel had also been thinned out a bit to allow more room for the stator to be mounted on the left-hand case. The tried-and-true Wide Glide fork was used right on through the final Shovelhead production in 1984 1/2.

"My Shovelhead rides like a big old Cadillac, kind of like bouncing on big bedsprings," said Jim Glazner, an Alabama man whose 1969 FLH is seen in this book. "I went nuts the first time I hit a big bump and went up in the air. It was a great feeling because you don't really feel it. You glide up and down on the shocks in the seat." He added that he was impressed at just how much power the torquey Shovelhead has. "You've got all kinds of torque on the low end. If you get down, it just pulls away in a major way, especially 40 to 60. It's just a 'bwaaaaa' and you're gone."

The Shovelhead FLHs were known for their sheer mass. In their day they demanded attention and they got it. But underneath all the saddlebags, Tour Pack, and windshield was a low, narrow motorcycle. No, nobody would confuse it with a back road burner, but an experienced rider back then could hustle them around well enough to put a little hurt on the footboards and primary cover. It was a stable, predictable machine that wouldn't turn around and bite you. You could load them to the hilt and ride them as long as you wanted. The engine was strong and had lots of torque, although the single wire non-

1970 FLH
The biggest change made by Harley-Davidson in 1970 was dropping the generator and going to an alternator, which required a completely different set of crankcases. A permanent magnet-type alternator was mounted to the lefthand crankcase, while a new timing cover, dubbed the "nose cone cover," replaced the former cover. The old-style circuit breaker also disappeared, replaced by a set of points.
Jeff Hackett

returning throttle—an early "cruise control"—used through 1973 could be an unwelcome feature at times to the unwary. One solid Big Twin feature was the clutch that had been used from 1941 to early 1984. A bit on the noisy side, yes, but reliable.

On the flip side, the brakes still weren't up to the job. An FL that weighed well over 700lb before you loaded it up and capable of flirting with 100mph needed better stoppers. The 1966–1971 model Shovelheads used the same single-leading-shoe drum brake that had been around since 1949. The first front disc brake FL models came out in 1972, with the same old hydraulic rear drum brake that had been used since 1958. The front disc brakes from 1972 to early 1980 were often a major headache because the caliper was large and heavy, the mount was inadequate and vibration could spell an early end to the mounting bushings.

"There were various anti-rattle repair kits offered, but they all amounted to a Band-Aid on a concussion," Heinrichs said. He noted that some riders would change the rear brake pistons because the rear brake "had a distressing tendency to heat up and apply

itself. No joke!" It wasn't until Harley went to the Girling rear brake caliper in 1981 that the braking woes were cured. A slightly improved version of the front brake soldiered on through 1984. The shift linkage, meanwhile, was on the sloppy side, which usually stemmed from wear between the shift lever and the gearbox. That resulted in a certain amount of excess motion, which made for long travel between shifts.

Meanwhile, something else was going on at Harley-Davidson, which had been bought out in 1969 by AMF. The new owners did not

1971 FX Super Glide
Other than a few tabs and mounts, the FL and FX frames were the same. Of course, the FX, with its XL front fork, also got some of the "Flexi-

Flyer" handling attributes, but it was a definite head turner and lots of fun for around-town blasting. Doug Mitchel

make many fans (a polite way of putting it), but the AMF folks were smart enough to let the Harley people handle the creative side of the business. Willie G. Davidson, grandson of one of the original Davidsons, was more than just an ace designer. He saw and understood what riders were doing outside the factory. The aftermarket business was thriving as customizers turned the beloved yet cumbersome FLs into the most outrageous mean, lean street machines. It was a tide that could not be turned, and Willie G. and Co. were smart enough not to try and turn it away.

The idea seems like a natural today. Harley-Davidson had proven winners in its classic FL line and its performance-minded Sportster line, but what that gave you was a choice of either a big heavy highway machine or the smaller, more spirited XL cruiser. A huge gap existed between the two.

Enter the 1971 FX, a combination of the sturdy FL frame and the streamlined XL front end. The Super Glide, as it was called, offered the FL's solid look yet weighing in some 70lb less, it had the lighter look and feel of the Sportster. Other than a few tabs and mounts, the FL and FX frames were the same. And even though some folks liked to refer to the Sportster front fork as a "Flexi-Flyer," the FX featured an improvement up front: it had fork seals, something the earlier XL forks had lacked. The FX front and rear drum brakes were not much to brag about, but you could blast the Super Glide around town and look awful good doing it. It was nimble, a head turner, and a monstrous success.

The Super Glide worked for a simple reason: it gave the people what they wanted. It was what the custom builders were doing, and Harley-Davidson coming out with it made

1971 FX Super Glide
The FX mated the sturdy FL frame with the streamlined XL front end. The Super Glide, as it was called, offered the FL's solid look yet weighing in 70lb less, and had the lighter look and feel of the Sportster. The front disc brakes were still around the corner, however, and the single-leading-shoe drum brake that had been used since 1949 still was only so-so.
Doug Mitchel

a lot of sense. Harley has always been a market-driven company, never long off the track when it came to what riders wanted. By no means does that mean that Harley would be the first one at the table with the new cutting-edge technology, and critics have noted that The Motor Company tended to squeeze every last possible drop out of its R&D and production lines, but it knew when to go forward. And with the Super Glide, Harley-Davidson found itself with a hit. It still looks good today, although you'd be hard pressed to find

1971 FX Super Glide
Until the FX came out in 1971, Harley riders had a choice between the large touring-bred FL line or the small sporty XL line. More riders were chopping their FLs into leaner machines, so Harley-Davidson decided that it could lead the way, which it did by doing a presto-chango to create the Super Glide. The FX was a hit, and led to new lines of hybrid Harleys such as the Low Rider and the Super Glide II, but the rather odd-looking one-piece fiberglass fender-seat base was definitely un-Harley like. A more traditional setup was used the next year. Doug Mitchel

many fans of the odd-looking one-piece fiberglass fender-seat base (a more traditional set-up was used the next year). The FX led to a slew of new hybrid Harleys such as the Low Rider, the Fat Bob, and the Super Glide II.

The demand was there, especially for the personalized-look Harleys. A few years earlier, in 1969, a low-budget B-grade film called *Easy Rider*, starring two unknowns, Peter Fonda and Dennis Hopper, struck a chord with motorcyclists. At the same time, the nation was at war with itself over its involvement in a far-off place called Vietnam. Large numbers of veterans back from Vietnam turned to Harley-Davidsons, much like their fathers did when they came back from World War II. The FX made perfect sense.

It's hard to measure a Harley in the traditional standards used for other brands. Maybe that's why it shouldn't be a surprise that the 1972 Super Glide got a curiously written lukewarm review from *Cycle World*, which described it as "a Sportster for those people who like 74s." The Super Glide was best traveling in a straight line and took some muscling to get through corners, they reported. The brakes were pretty bad and the bars, with a width of 28in, were too narrow. The reviewers praised the solid clutch, torque, and gas mileage (47mpg), but there seemed to be a lot more to pan, from the clunky shifting to the heavy vibration. With the Super Glide selling for $2,500, "The Sportster is, relatively speaking, a better value at about $2,100," the writers concluded.

It was nothing new for Harleys to be criticized in an era where the hallmark was set by smooth four-cylinder wonders. But the Super Glide fared especially poor, and in some part that may have been due to the times. It was the era of AMF when production numbers went to the sky and beyond (from 37,620 bikes built in 1971 to 59,908 in 1972 to 70,903 in 1973), and where Harley-Davidsons were being lambasted for problems right out of the showroom. Quality control was so bad at one point that C. E. Hodde, owner of Aggieland Harley-Davidson in Texas, recalled he was torn between selling and convincing prospective Harley owners *not* to buy a new

1980 FXWG Wide Glide
Right, what's that saying about imitation being the sincerest form of flattery? This 1960s FL-style Harley is actually a 1980 FXWG that was given the retro-look by its owner, Robert Timms, Jr. It's hard to argue against the late-Pan, early-Shovel styling, especially with that sharp trumpet horn. Kit Noble

1980 FXWG Wide Glide
Left, appearances can be deceiving. This 1980
Wide Glide FL-lookalike harbors a 100ci stroker,
S&S carburetor, Sifton cam, and dual plug setup
(the second coil is hidden in the toolbox).
Kit Noble

1980 FXWG Wide Glide
Above, the correct paint scheme for this look
Harley would have the white below the red on
the tank and fenders. But the owner, Robert
Timms, Jr, was the painter, and this is how he
wanted it. Kit Noble

1980 FXSB Sturgis Low Rider
Other than the fact that it shouldn't be wearing those buckhorn bars, this 1980 FXSB Sturgis Low Rider is basically stock. The Sturgis stunned the riding community with its primary and final belt drives, which received a cautious reception from some riders who preferred to trust their fate to a chain. Didn't matter. The return to the belt-drive system was on its way. The Sturgis made extensive use of black paint that added to its unique look. Its high-compression engine wasn't easy to kick over, but once you did, it ran strong, clocking 106mph at one Cycle World *test. Roy Kidney*

bike from him. "I knew the sum' bitch would be back to be fixed, and I'd have to make good on it out of my pocket."

OK, so it was not necessarily the best of times for new Harley-Davidsons. But that didn't seem to be the problem with the *Cycle World* testers. They just didn't see the attraction. Not that they spelled it out quite that way. The review acknowledged that the Super Glide would do well with the Harley crowd, but the unspoken implication was that some folks just don't know any better. The problem is that their tests didn't allow a criteria for something the average Harley rider in the street could have told them: what

makes a Harley so special is the "all's right with the world" good feeling you get from firing one up and riding it, and vibration and so-so brakes—and even some screwups at the factory that have to be fixed—don't make it less of a Harley.

What made the FX so right was the approach, the statement it made. Harley riders thought enough of the FX to buy it in droves. Production the first year was 4,700, bumped up to 6,500 in 1972, and 7,625 the following year. The 1973 Super Glide got a Kayaba fork, and even though the fork had the same caliper as the FL models, it was still a big improvement over the earlier fork and brake.

The FXE came out in 1974, and it settled any doubts that Harley riders would take to an electric start if given a choice. Kicking your beast to life may be satisfying, but the FXE (E for electric) outsold the FX by a two-to-one margin, a ratio that tripled the following year (9,350 to 3,060). The FXE got a new first gear to replace the old "stump puller" 3.0:1 first gear ratio. The Liberty Edition FXE came out in 1976, and featured a Bicentennial special black metalflake paint job with red, white, and blue touches.

During all these changes, the Shovelhead gearbox was essentially the same system that came out in 1936, and aside from a different case in 1965 (two outriggers were added to the casting to support the cast-aluminum inner primary) it went through 1977 before any significant changes were made. That year, the loose roller bearings for the main drive gear were replaced by a caged-bearing assembly, which meant a new main drive gear was needed. Also, the loose bearings in the countershaft were replaced by caged needle bearings.

Taking the basic idea of two into one equals something new, magical, and marketable, Harley-Davidson went another step in 1977 with the FXS, which was the first factory motorcycle that riders didn't sit on, they wore. It came in your choice of one color—gun metal gray. A Harley habit of sorts is that when a new model comes out, customers normally don't get a lot of choices when it comes to color. With a seat height of under 28in and a 19in wheel up front and a 16in wheel in back, the FXS earned its tag, the Low Rider. Style by its very nature means change, but if there is one enduring feature of custom Harley-Davidsons that seems unlikely to fade away into distant memories it's a low-sitting machine. You sat deep into it, kicked your legs high out front on the highway pegs, and rode off with an inherent promise of adventure and romance. The

1967 Electra Glide
This 1967 Electra Glide has received the aftermarket treatment in several ways—from the passenger floorboard to the paint—turning it into a fine-looking machine. Roy Kidney

1967 Electra Glide
Harley-Davidson experimented with various front bumpers over the year, even using plastic in the past couple years. Roy Kidney

Low Rider offered that and more.

With its extended Showa front fork, stiff rear shocks, and short handlebars, the Low Rider was not meant to be an easy around town rider. It took a good rider to prove that the 5.4in of ground clearance could be put to full use, and the twin disc brakes up front looked good, but they didn't provide as much stopping power as their looks promised although they did help you develop a strong right hand grip. But that didn't change the results. The Low Rider, with its Morris cast wheels and black finish touches on the cases, heads, and barrels, was style personified. A total of 3,742 Low Riders were produced in 1977, and when the Harley-Davidson execs looked at what they had, they upped production the next year to nearly 10,000.

Following a bigger is better approach, Harley-Davidson came out with an 80ci engine in 1978 1/2. The 80 was simply the old 74ci with a little more bore and a lot more stroke. The old 74ci had a 3 7/16in bore and a 3 31/32in stroke all the way from 1941 through 1980. The 80ci engine now measured 3 1/2x4 1/4in. The 80ci cylinder got a new head-style bolt and base nut and washer arrangement, which can be used on any 74ci or 80ci ohv from 1941 to 1984 1/2. You can tell the older cylinders because they have a part number ending in a 66 on the base flange while the newer ones end in a 78. By 1981, the 74ci engine was retired, the same way as it had sent the 64ci engine packing.

The 80ci engine, which had a lower compression ratio (from 8.0:1 to 7.4:1), was a hit and so was the Low Rider, but Harley-Davidson didn't stop for long. In 1979, the Fat Bob was introduced. The Fat Bob FXEF was really a Super Glide Low Rider with twin gas tanks, buckhorn bars, and your choice of cast or spoke wheels, with a 74ci or an 80ci engine. Chalk up another hit. Sales were 4,678 for the 74ci FXEF, 5,264 for the 80ci version.

Harley-Davidson, clearly in the winner's seat with the FX line, kept it going in 1980 with the introduction of the Sturgis, a Low Rider designated the FXB. The B designation stood for belt, as in belt drive, but what was amazing about the first FXB is that it featured not just a final belt drive but a primary belt as well.

The toothed rubber belts, obviously wider than a chain, were not an easy fit. The starter mechanism had to be played with to work with the belts and new sprockets. The spring-loaded compensator sprocket was replaced by a new sprocket, which has rubber dampers inside. Why the move to belts? Belts last far longer, require less maintenance, and reduce vibration, but the Sturgis model was not what you call an instant success in that regard. If you had to change the belt turning your rear wheel, you had to pull the final primary belt first. Also, there were still no lack of Harley purists who liked the idea of chain drive and rode around with a spare master link, just in case. The FXB cost $5,687, a little more than $250 more than the chain-drive Low Rider.

1983 FXSB Wide Glide
Riders had already been customizing Harley-Davidsons for ages, but during the Shovelhead era it became easier than ever to take a stock Harley and make it into a custom ride, as with this 1983 FXSB Wide Glide owned by Brian

McCormick of Pennsylvania. The idea was, and for many riders continues to be, that Harley provided you a building block. It's up to you to build on it. Jeff Hackett

1983 FXSB Wide Glide
There's more aftermarket than stock parts on Brian McCormick's 1983 FXSB. The S&S Teardrop air cleaner, SU II carburetor, Iso pegs, drag pipes, extra chrome, and other assorted fine touches are nice additions to the stock cycle.
Jeff Hackett

The Sturgis, with its belt-drive system, featured a new transmission case and a change in gear ratios, most notably second gear. The Sturgis had the most highway-friendly ratio gearing of any Harley, with a top final ratio of 3.27:1, compared to 3.42:1 for the Low Rider models and 3.36:1 for the Tour Glide. All of which meant that the Sturgis was able to putt along quite comfortably on the highway. As with all things, there is a price to pay, and in this case the highway gearing translated to a slightly pokey quarter-mile time of 14.64 seconds at 91.18mph in a *Cycle World* test. Then again, the Low Rider was not made for dragstrip launches, and its gas mileage (48mpg) meant that the

3 1/2 gallon tank could take you about as far as you would want to go without taking a break.

That same year, Harley-Davidson proved that yes, you can go back to the well real soon—that is, if you have something that will make folks want to drink up, and that they had in the FXWG. The Wide Glide, as it was called, was simply the most customized-looking bike ever put out by a factory. Complete with a flamed paint job, extended front fork, and 21in wheel up front, the Wide Glide was a stunning machine. It looked like something that came right out of a custom bike shop; the Low Rider formula had been taken further than anyone ever expected possible.

Being the real world, there was some unhappiness going on in Harleyland, and it really wasn't the company's fault—but it was their problem to deal with. By mid-1978, the emission control demon had come to visit and made life miserable in the form of sticking valves. To meet the Federal mandate, Harley had to use a leaner air-fuel mixture. At the same time, the oil companies began reducing the amount of lead in its fuel. That combination led to a lot of problems, such as the joy of pinging. The factory responded by changing the old-style steel valve guides to a new larger diameter (0.625in instead of 0.564in) cast-iron guide. Harley also began using a "hard" valve with the stems hardened by carburizing or hard chroming. At the same time, The Motor Company also changed the intake manifold flange from a double-lip to single-lip type. (The older heads had used a round intake manifold "O" ring. The later models used a flat or "rubber band" seal. The early heads and manifolds will accommodate either style; the late cylinder heads only the large-style seat).

It was a good effort, but the sticking valve problem continued. One reason was that the 1980 guide was shorter than the earlier guide. That caused an unacceptable rate of guide wear, and a lot of smoke and stuck valves due to carbon buildup. That "sticky" situation was ended in 1981 through the use of longer valve guides (still cast iron and still 0.625in) and the addition of a valve guide seal. Those changes not only ended the stuck valve problem, but substantially reduced oil consumption.

The aftermarket sector now supplies cast-iron guides, "hard" valves, and guide seals to fit Big Twins back to 1948. The early Shovelhead intake manifolds were made of cast iron, although you can replace them with the aluminum ones used in later models. All the Shovelhead cylinders were made of cast iron. The early cylinder models, 1966–1978, had a thinner base flange and one more fin (a total of ten) than the later-style cylinder (1978 1/2–1984 1/2), which had a thick base flange and nine fins.

Meanwhile, while the FX line was drawing in all kinds of attention and new riders, the FL line was quietly motoring along with modest changes. The FL was discontinued after 1979 in favor of its more heavily loaded big brother, the FLH, which offered an incredibly wide range of standard equipment. That same year, you could order an FLHC with a sidecar.

In 1980, Harley updated the traditional Harley touring machine with the introduction of the FLT Tour Glide. This was not just a minor upgrade—it was a whole new machine, a motorcycle that had been designed to be an integrated unit. It featured a new welded-steel frame, a rectangular steel backbone with two downtubes that

was stiffer than its FL counterpart. The drivetrain was connected to the frame through a three-point elastomer mounting system designed to isolate the rider from vibration. The shakes would still be there, but you wouldn't feel it.

The Tour Glide, which sold for just over $6,000, was not only lighter than the FLH, it had 2in more ground clearance, and featured a new swing arm that, combined with repositioned shocks, allowed for more wheel travel. The FLT weighed in at 752lb with a half tank of gas. It featured a five-speed transmission with a final gear that made for lower engine rpm for highway cruising. The Tour Glide came with an enclosed final chain drive so it ran in oil, not grit, and there was a spin-on oil filter that made that maintenance chore easier. The fairing was now mounted on the frame, and you couldn't help but notice the two big, big headlights. The FLT's exhaust had a different look. Instead of the front and rear pipes snaking back from the right side, the exhaust pipe for the front cylinder twisted back inside the frame on the left side, over the primary case and back out to a muffler on the left side. (If you flip through just about any Harley-Davidson magazine, you'll notice that if there's only one full-picture shot, invariably it will be from the right side because that view—the exhaust and carb/air cleaner—is considered the most aesthetically pleasing.)

Although lighter than the FL, the Tour Glide offered lots of room for stowage space. You could still get the spring seat as an option, but the lower-sitting solid seat was more popular. The V-Fire ignition (replaced by the V-Fire II in 1981) provided a better spark without points. The instruments were no longer tank mounted, but were instead located in a single cluster between the bars. The fork tubes were offset 4 degrees, 15 degrees from the steering head for better trail. Up front, double 10in discs handled the stopping chores with a 12in disc at the rear. *Cycle World* reviewers declared that it should be given "The Most Improved Motorcycle" award, praising the effectiveness of the engine-mounting system, 400lb load capability, overall quiet ride (a Harley?), and passenger comfort.

By 1981, AMF was out of the motorcycle business, courtesy of a Harley-Davidson employee buyout led by a cadre of officials. The move back to private ownership was welcomed, but it didn't prevent the company from falling into its most precarious fiscal situation ever. But that didn't prevent the introduction of another model, the Super Glide II, a long, long (64.7in wheelbase) lean machine that weighed in at just over 600lb with a half tank of gas.

The 1982 FXRS/FXR featured the FLT-style vibration isolating mount system, but the frame was not the same as the Tour Glide. It was far stiffer than the FLFT's, and even though a few Harley purists thought the frame looked too much like a foreign unit, the computer-designed frame was Harley through and through. Another plus with the 1982 models was that the compression had been lowered and regular gas could be used.

With a selling price under $7,000 and a top end of about 100mph (a *Cycle World* test showed it doing the quarter-mile in 14.26 seconds at 91.46mph), the FXR series was not a speed demon, yet it was the answer for riders who loved the chopper look but also wanted a little less on the vibration.

The FXRS model came with a few more bells and whistles than the FXR, such as highway pegs, cast wheels and a sissy bar, but both shared the same improvements. The Girling rear disc brake combined with the twin discs up front, with the help of a new master cylinder, offered decent stopping power. With its low center of gravity and long wheelbase, the FXR series was good at cornering. Harley introduced the FXRT, a touring version, the next year. It was meant to be smaller than the FLT, and came with a real anti-dive system.

The Evo engine retired the Shovelhead's eighteen-year run; the last Shovelhead engine was assembled in June 1984. The Evo had the same crankcases and same displacement and cylinder size, but the top end was all new and better. It was progress, and much appreciated progress at that. The reliable Evo engine made owning and riding a Harley that much easier. It's been out for more than a decade now, and no doubt it too will eventually be replaced. But all that doesn't change some basic ideas. As Wally Mitchell put it above, "Harleys today don't do anything more than they used to do," he insisted. "You get on them and ride them, and that makes you someone special." Well put, Wally.

1983 FXSB Wide Glide
How successful was Harley-Davidson's FX with riders? The FX line debuted in 1971 with the basic FX (4,700 built), but by 1983, Harley had learned to mix'n'match the FX and FL so well that the lineup included the FXE (1,215 made), FXWG (2,873), FXSSB (3,277), FXDG (810), FXR (1,069), FXRS (1,413), and the FXRT (1,458). And if you know what all those Harley codes stand for, you are a wise person indeed. Jeff Hackett

Index